Hail Lord Ganesha!

My Culture My Identity!

Thakur Rudra Pratap Singh

Simplified Version of the actual

Preface

"India is a country of Sanatan (Hindu) religion. Where Ganesha and Brahma are the incarnations of Vishnu, Mahesh and is revered.

Respect Hinduism, make this eternal country your identity."

Simplified Version of the actual

Let's say together –

"Let there be harmony among beings,

Hail Goddess Durga!

Har Har Mahadev

Hail Sanatan Dharma!

India was of Hindus and will remain of Hindus forever!

Bharat Mata Ki Jai!"

(The Hindi version of the book is also out and is available for sale on internet).

Thakur Rudra Pratap Singh is a 15-year-old distinguished figure known for his exceptional contributions to science, technology, and literature. He serves as a Scientist Apprentice with NASA and ISRO, with experience as an Astrophysics Apprentice at the

University of Hawaii and Hardin-Simmons University. As a researcher affiliated with IIT Kanpur and IIT Bhubaneswar, he has written multiple research papers. Singh is also a world record holder as the youngest author of juvenile fiction and a Member of Parliament in the World Teen Parliament. His innovative work and dedication to education make him a recognized global young leader in science and social causes.

Contents

1	Indian Culture	9
2	ChampakRaman Pillai	24
3	Nehru's True Identity	36
4	Mughals ruined India.	46
5	Don't lose B.J.P	57
6	Vishwaguru Bharat	68
7	Protector of Hinduism	81
8	Something not right	110

Simplified Version of the actual

The content in this book incorporates references from reliable sources such as Wikipedia, WikiHow, Citizendium, MSN, and others to ensure accuracy and relevance. All material has been utilized in strict compliance with the terms and conditions of the respective platforms, with no intention of infringing on copyrights.

.1.

Our Indian Culture

Our culture is our identity. Among the defining aspects of a nation's identity, culture holds a paramount place. For centuries, India has been celebrated on the global stage for its rich cultural heritage and traditions. However, in the present era, this legacy appears to be under threat. Several detrimental changes in Indian culture are indicative of this alarming trend.

Indian culture has long been synonymous with the ethos of "**Atithi Devo Bhava**" (the guest is God). Yet, in recent years, incidents of sexual violence against foreign tourists, particularly women, have tarnished this reputation. Similarly, the spirit of "**Vasudhaiva Kutumbakam**" (the world is one family), which traditionally defined Indian society, seems to be waning. Regional, state, and communal divisions have fragmented the unity that once characterized the nation. India, celebrated for its "**unity in diversity,**" now grapples with divisions fueled by religion and other sectarian differences.

Kabir, the great poet-saint, once said, *"India is a nation where*

Hindus and Muslims draw water from the same ghats; it is my privilege to be born in such a nation." Festivals like Holi, Diwali, Eid, and Ramzan were once celebrated by all Indians as national occasions, transcending religious boundaries. Muslims would burst crackers during Diwali, and Hindus would wish their Muslim friends "Eid Mubarak." Unfortunately, this harmonious coexistence has been overshadowed by communal riots and violence, where innocents have become victims of divisive ideologies.

The culture of sages and seers that once flourished has, in some cases, been undermined by hypocritical and fraudulent spiritual leaders. Similarly, the

Indian pride in the Hindi language has diminished, with many shying away from speaking it. The Ramayana and the Bhagavad Gita, once central to Indian households, are now found in only a few homes. Sanskrit, the ancient language of India, is understood and spoken by only a select few in isolated pockets. The vibrant village tradition of elders gathering at the *chaupals* (village meeting places) has largely disappeared, along with the practice of seeking blessings by touching elders' feet.

India, a nation once known for its unwavering commitment to "Ahimsa Paramo Dharma" (non-violence is the highest duty), has witnessed disturbing episodes of violence in recent years. These incidents have left the world questioning whether this is the same land where a peace-loving ambassador like Mahatma Gandhi once preached the message of non-violence.

Despite these challenges, India continues to showcase its cultural prowess on the global stage. By introducing yoga to the world, India reaffirmed its status as a "Vishwa Guru" (world teacher). Indian culture, with its profound depth and inclusivity, remains immortal. However, its identity is at risk of being eroded by certain actions and behaviors that cast a shadow over its legacy.

In this age of materialism, we must remain vigilant to preserve our cultural heritage. It is not enough to merely save it; we must actively nurture and promote it so that future generations can carry forward its timeless essence. Our culture is not just a relic of the past but a beacon for the future, guiding us to live with dignity, unity, and purpose.

Indian culture holds special significance in the history of the world from many points of view. It is one of the oldest civilizations and continues to fascinate people worldwide. Traditionally, Indian families emphasize arranged marriages, where unions are often decided by parents or other respected family members with the consent of both the bride and groom. Factors like family background, caste, and horoscope compatibility are typically considered in these arrangements. Marriage in India is viewed as a lifelong commitment, with the divorce rate remaining remarkably low at around 1% compared to 50% in the United States. This figure is even lower for arranged marriages. However, the divorce rate has been gradually increasing, sparking varied opinions: traditionalists view this as societal disintegration, while modernists see it as an indicator of women's empowerment.

Despite child marriage being outlawed in 1860, the practice persists in some regions, with reports indicating that 24% of girls are married before the age of 18. Disturbingly, 40% of the world's child marriages occur in

India. Efforts are ongoing to combat this issue, but challenges remain. Indian naming conventions are diverse and influenced by religion, caste, and epics, reflecting the country's rich cultural tapestry.

Women in India often bear the responsibility of household chores and community service. Although legal reforms ensure equal property rights for women, enforcement remains weak, particularly in rural areas, where women face nutritional discrimination and are prone to anemia and malnourishment. Rangoli, a traditional art form, is popular among Indian women and symbolizes cultural expression. Magazines like Femina and Women's Era cater specifically to women's interests.

Cows hold a sacred position in Indian society, particularly in Hindu-majority regions like India and Nepal. Cow slaughter is prohibited in most Indian states, except West Bengal and Kerala, and harming a cow can lead to imprisonment. Cows are often seen roaming freely, even in bustling cities like Delhi. Milk plays a vital role in religious rituals and daily life, reflecting the deep reverence for these animals.

Namaste, a traditional greeting, signifies respect and is used across India and Nepal. In yoga, it embodies a spiritual connection, translating to "The light within me bows to the light within you." This gesture is performed with palms pressed together and fingers pointing upwards, a symbol of humility and reverence.

Festivals in India reflect its multicultural and multi-religious fabric. Diwali, the festival of lights, is celebrated with diyas and rangolis. Other notable festivals include Holi, Navratri, Eid, and Christmas. Harvest festivals like Pongal and Onam emphasize the agricultural roots of Indian culture. The Kumbh Mela, a massive Hindu pilgrimage, draws millions of devotees, showcasing the spiritual fervor of the nation.

Indian cuisine is diverse and deeply rooted in regional and cultural traditions. Known for its complex use of spices, Indian food includes vegetarian staples like rice and lentils, as well as non-vegetarian dishes featuring chicken, goat, lamb, and fish. Meals are often communal, fostering social cohesion. Culinary influences from the Mughals and Europeans have enriched the gastronomic landscape, making Indian cuisine globally renowned.

Traditional Indian attire varies across regions, with sarees, salwar kameez, and dhotis being prominent. Bollywood, the unofficial name for India's film industry based in Mumbai, is the world's largest producer of films. Besides commercial cinema, acclaimed filmmakers like Satyajit Ray and Guru Dutt have contributed significantly to the art of filmmaking. The advent of multiplexes and global exposure has diversified audience preferences, leading to the growth of niche cinema.

Indian philosophy has profoundly influenced global thought, particularly in the East. Concepts like zero, introduced via Arab mediation, underscore India's scientific and mathematical legacy. Ancient schools of thought like Buddhism, Jainism, and materialism emerged alongside Greek philosophies. Modern philosophers like Swami Vivekananda and Rabindranath Tagore have continued India's intellectual tradition, advocating democracy, secularism, and liberalism. Nobel laureate Amartya Sen exemplifies India's contribution to contemporary economics.

India's religious diversity is evident in its demographic composition:

Religion	Population	%
Sanatan	827,578,868	80%
Muslim	138,188,240	13%
Christian	24,080,016	2%
Sikh	19,215,730	1.8%
Buddhist	7,955,207	0.7%
Jain	4,225,053	0.4%
Other	6,639,626	0.6%
Not stated	727,588	0.1%

Radio broadcasting began in India in 1927 and evolved into All India Radio (AIR), a government-run service. The liberalization of the 1990s allowed private FM and AM broadcasters, transforming radio into a diverse and dynamic medium. Indian television, introduced in 1959, gained momentum during the 1982 Asian Games, which marked the advent of color broadcasting. Popular series like Ramayana and Mahabharata revolutionized Indian television. Today, the small screen thrives with diverse programming, catering to varied audiences and creating opportunities for aspiring actors and filmmakers.

Simplified Version of the actual

.2.
C.R. Pillai

Champak Raman Pillai, born on September 15, 1891, in Thiruvananthapuram, Travancore, was a dedicated freedom fighter whose contributions to India's independence struggle, despite being far from home, have often been overlooked. From his early education in Thiruvananthapuram, he soon found himself drawn into revolutionary circles during his time in Europe.

Introduced to Sir Walter Strickland, a British biologist, while still in school, Pillai's journey to Europe was serendipitous. Strickland took him to Austria, where Pillai completed his high school education. This exposure to Europe's political atmosphere marked the beginning of his transformation into a passionate freedom fighter. He soon joined the technical institute for engineering studies, but the growing global conflict of World War I ignited his nationalist fervor. It was during this time that he founded the 'International Pro-India Committee' in Zurich in 1914, aiming to unite overseas Indians in the fight for freedom from British rule.

Pillai's involvement deepened when he moved to Berlin in 1914 and merged his committee with the 'Indian Independence Committee'. The committee's mission was to engage in revolutionary activities, seeking German support to overthrow British colonialism in India. This collaboration led to the so-called 'Hindu-German conspiracy,' which aimed to undermine British rule using Germany's resources during the war. Notably, Pillai is believed to have coined the iconic slogan 'Jai Hind,' which became synonymous with India's fight for freedom.

In 1915, following the establishment of a Provisional Government of India in Kabul by King Mahendra Pratap and Mohammad Barkatullah, Pillai was appointed the Foreign Minister of this government. His role in the government was pivotal as he worked to secure international support for India's independence. Unfortunately, the defeat of Germany in World War I led to the expulsion of the revolutionaries from Afghanistan, and the movement faced setbacks.

Despite these challenges, Pillai continued his revolutionary activities, meeting with Subhas Chandra Bose in Vienna in 1919, where they discussed plans for India's independence. Although his efforts were often overshadowed by the larger movements of the time, his dedication remained unwavering.

In his personal life, Champak Raman Pillai married Lakshmibai from Manipur in 1931. Sadly, after their marriage, he fell seriously ill, and it is suspected that he was poisoned while receiving treatment in Italy. Pillai died on May 28, 1934, in Berlin. His wife, Lakshmibai, brought his ashes back to India, where they were honored with full state recognition in Kanyakumari.

Champak Raman Pillai's story is one of immense sacrifice and dedication to the cause of Indian independence. His contributions, often overshadowed by other prominent leaders, continue to inspire those who believe in the power of revolutionary spirit and the fight for justice.

This revision focuses on summarizing Champak Raman Pillai's life and revolutionary contributions in a single chapter format, reflecting the key events and impacts.

Champak Raman Pillai, born on September 15, 1891, in Thiruvananthapuram, Travancore, was a dedicated freedom fighter whose contributions to India's independence struggle, despite being far from home, have often been overlooked. From his early education in Thiruvananthapuram, he soon found himself drawn into revolutionary circles during his time in Europe.

Introduced to Sir Walter Strickland, a British biologist, while still in school, Pillai's journey to Europe was serendipitous. Strickland took him to Austria, where Pillai completed his high school education. This exposure to Europe's political atmosphere marked the beginning of his transformation into a passionate freedom fighter. He soon joined the technical institute for engineering studies, but the growing global conflict of World War I ignited his nationalist fervor. It was during this time that he founded the 'International Pro-India Committee' in Zurich in 1914, aiming to unite overseas Indians in the fight for freedom from British rule.

Pillai's involvement deepened when he moved to Berlin in 1914 and merged his committee with the 'Indian Independence Committee'. The committee's mission was to engage in revolutionary activities, seeking German support to overthrow British colonialism in India. This collaboration led to the so-called 'Hindu-German conspiracy,' which aimed to undermine British rule using Germany's resources during the war. Notably, Pillai is believed to have coined the iconic slogan 'Jai Hind,' which became synonymous with India's fight for freedom.

In 1915, following the establishment of a Provisional Government of India in Kabul by King Mahendra Pratap and Mohammad Barkatullah, Pillai was appointed the Foreign Minister of this government. His role in the government was pivotal as he worked to secure international support for India's independence. Unfortunately, the defeat of Germany in World War I led to the expulsion of the revolutionaries from Afghanistan, and the movement faced setbacks.

Despite these challenges, Pillai continued his revolutionary activities, meeting with Subhas Chandra Bose in Vienna in 1919, where they discussed plans for India's independence. Although his efforts were often overshadowed by the larger movements of the time, his dedication remained unwavering.

In his personal life, Champak Raman Pillai married Lakshmibai from Manipur in 1931. Sadly, after their marriage, he fell seriously ill, and it is suspected that he was poisoned while receiving treatment in Italy. Pillai died on May 28, 1934, in Berlin. His wife, Lakshmibai, brought his ashes back to India, where they were honored with full state recognition in Kanyakumari.

Champak Raman Pillai's story is one of immense sacrifice and dedication to the cause of Indian independence. His contributions, often overshadowed by other prominent leaders, continue to inspire those who believe in the power of revolutionary spirit and the fight for justice.

Simplified Version of the actual

.3.
Nehru Family

In the political narrative of India, the Nehru-Gandhi family has stood as one of the most influential dynasties. From the days of Jawaharlal Nehru, India's first Prime Minister, to the leadership of his daughter, Indira Gandhi, and her descendants, the family has played a crucial role in shaping the nation's destiny. However, the family's origins and its religious identity have often been the subject of intrigue and debate.

Rahul Gandhi: Hindu, Muslim, or Parsi?

Recently, Rahul Gandhi, in an attempt to appeal to the voters in Gujarat during the 2022 Assembly elections, visited the Somnath Temple, proclaiming himself a "family Hindu" with faith in temples. Yet, this display of religious devotion raised questions about his true religious identity. Critics argue that his temple visits are just political gestures meant for electoral gain, as he is rarely seen in temples outside of election time.

Furthermore, questions about Rahul Gandhi's identity have arisen, not just due to his public behavior but also due to his family's complex history. His paternal grandmother, Indira

Gandhi, had a Parsi heritage, which adds another layer to the family's diverse background. This revelation has sparked further discussion about his true religious beliefs—whether he is a Hindu, a Muslim, or a Parsi.

The Origins of the Nehru Family

The Nehru family's roots trace back to Kashmir. Jawaharlal Nehru himself shared in his autobiography that his ancestors were brought to Delhi in the early 1700s by the Mughal emperor Farrukhsier. The family gained prominence when they settled near a canal in Chandni Chowk, after which they became known by the name "Nehru."

Nehru's grandfather, Gangadhar Nehru, served as the Kotwal (chief of police) of Delhi just before the First War of Indian Independence in 1857. This period was catastrophic for the Nehru family, as the Ghadar (rebellion) led to the destruction of many prominent families, including theirs. The family's documents were destroyed, and they were forced to leave Delhi and relocate to Agra, where Motilal Nehru, Jawaharlal's father, was born.

The Rise of the Political Dynasty

Motilal Nehru, despite not being highly educated, carved out a successful career as a lawyer and became involved in India's freedom struggle. His political journey paved the way for the family's involvement in Indian politics. Through his advocacy work in Allahabad, Motilal gained substantial wealth and influence, allowing his son Jawaharlal Nehru to inherit a prominent political position.

Motilal Nehru was a key figure in the Indian National Congress, and it was through his political efforts that the Nehru-Gandhi family's political legacy began. His son, Jawaharlal Nehru, went on to become one of the most significant leaders in India's independence movement. As the first Prime Minister of India, Nehru was deeply involved in shaping the nation's future. His closeness to Mahatma Gandhi played a pivotal role in his rise to power.

The Role of Muslims in the Nehru Family's History

The Nehru family's connection to Muslims is significant, especially when considering the role that Muslims played in protecting them during the turmoil of 1857. Gangadhar Nehru's family was safeguarded by Muslim allies during the rebellion, and the family's survival can be attributed to their protection by the Muslim community. This historical context adds to the complexity of the Nehru family's identity and their connections to different religious communities.

Feroze Gandhi and the Family Legacy

Feroze Gandhi, the husband of Indira Gandhi, also played a pivotal role in the family's legacy.

Feroze, originally from a different background, had a strong relationship with the Nehru family. He took care of Indira Gandhi's mother, Kamala Nehru, during her illness, cementing his place within the family's inner circle.

Feroze Gandhi's contributions were essential in shaping the political future of the family. His legacy, however, would later intertwine with the Nehru-Gandhi dynasty, as his children—Indira Gandhi's sons—would continue to play a significant role in India's politics.

Conclusion: The Roots of the Dynasty

The Nehru-Gandhi family's history is not just one of political success, but also one of complex religious and cultural identities. From their Kashmiri origins to their association with Mughal-era India, the family has lived through significant historical moments that have shaped its current status. Their political dominance, built on the foundation laid by Motilal Nehru and carried forward by Jawaharlal Nehru, has remained largely intact, influencing Indian politics for generations.

Despite the family's claims of being a Hindu family, its historical ties to Muslims and Parsis remain an integral part of its story. This duality continues to define the Nehru-Gandhi family, as they balance their political power with the complexities of their identity.

As the family continues to play a role in India's political landscape, their past remains a topic of intrigue and debate.

Simplified Version of the actual

.4.

Mughals & India

Some people claim that India belongs to people of all religions, and others argue that India was ruled by the Mughals, so it belongs to the Muslims. The current situation is well-known, especially as investigations into various mosques reveal marks of Hindutva. There are numerous places in India that we claim to have built, but historically, many temples and cultural landmarks have been destroyed or repurposed by foreign invaders.

Take, for example, the Taj Mahal. While history tells us that Akbar built it for Mumtaz, there is a more complex story hidden beneath. The Taj Mahal was constructed on the remains of a revered Mahadev temple, and Akbar built a white marble structure over it for his wife. Even today, despite knowing the true origins, we still visit the Taj Mahal, forgetting the temple that once stood there.

Another poignant example is the Gyanvapi Mosque in Varanasi. A recent survey has revealed a Shiva temple beneath the mosque, making it part of the Kashi Vishwanath complex. Despite this discovery, there is resistance to acknowledging the truth, and many people hesitate to speak out about such issues. My intention with this book is to encourage people to raise their voices and promote our cultural heritage.

Survey of Gyanvapi Mosque and Evidence of Shiva Temple

The survey of the Gyanvapi Mosque in Varanasi was completed on May 16, 2022. According to the Hindu side, the survey found a Shivalinga in the Wuzukhana, which is part of the mosque. The Muslim side, however, claims no such discovery was made. The Hindu side has also presented five pieces of evidence linking the mosque to a Shiva temple:

1. **Shivlinga Found in Wuzukhana:** After the survey, the Hindu side claimed to have found a Shivalinga, which is significant because it suggests the mosque was built on a temple.

2. **Nandi's Direction:** The Hindu side argues that the Nandi's face in the temple complex faces the Shivalinga, supporting the theory that this was once a temple dedicated to Lord Shiva.

3. **Temple-like Structure of the Mosque:** The design and structure of the Gyanvapi Mosque resemble that of a Hindu temple, further supporting the claim that a temple once existed there.

4. **Bell Shapes on the Western Wall:** The walls of the mosque are adorned with bell-like shapes, a feature rarely seen in mosque architecture but common in Hindu temples.

5. **Document of Aurangzeb's Courtier:** Historical records from Aurangzeb's time mention the destruction of the temple and the subsequent construction of a mosque.

Destruction of Temples Across India

Historian Sita Ram Goel, along with Arun Shourie, Harsh Narayan, Jai Dubashi, and Ram Swaroop, uncovered the widespread destruction of temples during the Mughal period in their book *Hindu Temples: What Happened to Them?* This book chronicles over 1,800 mosques and other structures built by Muslims using the remains of destroyed temples. The book reveals that many of India's most famous historical sites, from the Qutub Minar to the Babri Masjid, were constructed in this way.

State-wise Evidence of Temple Destruction by the Mughals

Andhra Pradesh:

In this region, the authors list 142 sites where temples were demolished and replaced with mosques, including the Jami Masjid in Kadiri and the Babaya Dargah in Penukonda. Many other mosques and dargahs were built on the ruins of temples.

Assam:

In Assam, the Poa Masjid and the Mazaar of Sultan Ghiyasuddin Balban were constructed on the remains of temples. Both sites in Kamrup district are still revered as mosques and mazars today.

West Bengal:

West Bengal has a staggering 102 sites where mosques, dargahs, and forts were built on temple ruins. These include the Ghazi Ismail Mazar in Lokpura, which was built by destroying the Venugopal Temple. Several other mosques in the region were constructed using temple materials.

Bihar:

In Bihar, 77 places are identified where mosques and Muslim structures were built by demolishing temples. For example, in Bhagalpur, the dargah of Hazrat Shahbaz was built on the site of a temple, and in Champanagar, Jain temples were destroyed to make way for mazars.

Delhi:

The book mentions 72 places in Delhi where Muslim rulers destroyed temples to build seven cities. The Qutub Minar, Kuvvatul Islam Masjid, and several other monuments were constructed using temple materials.

Gujarat:

In Gujarat, 170 mosques were constructed on the ruins of temples. Notable sites include the temples of Aswal, Patan, and Chandravati, which were destroyed and used as building materials for mosques.

The Role of British and Muslim Historians

In their book, the authors also highlight how historians, both British and Muslim, have either justified or glorified the destruction of Hindu temples. British historians often defended the colonial regime, downplaying the brutalities committed by the Mughals, while Muslim historians celebrated the conquest and destruction of Hindu cultural heritage.

The inscriptions found on many mosques and historical buildings across India reveal details about how and when these structures were constructed, often citing Allah, the Prophet, and the Quran. These records, published by the Archaeological Survey of

India, provide crucial evidence of the systematic destruction of temples during the Mughal period.

Conclusion

The destruction of temples and the repurposing of their materials for the construction of mosques, forts, and other structures by the Mughals has been a widespread phenomenon throughout India. From the Qutub Minar to the Babri Masjid, the Gyanvapi Mosque, and beyond, this book uncovers the hidden history of India's cultural devastation. It is time for us to recognize these truths and reclaim our heritage, preserving and promoting the rich cultural and religious traditions that define our nation.

Simplified Version of the actual

.5.

B.J.P

In the near future, India will truly emerge as a Vishwaguru, recognized globally for its wisdom and leadership. Our country's identity abroad has been steadily rising, yet at the same time, we are witnessing an increasing adoption of Western lifestyles. This disparity is disheartening. The world sees us as a nation of knowledge and tradition, but we are veering towards foreign practices. Our youth sing Western tunes, wear foreign clothes, and speak languages like English and French. But let me ask you this:

Have you ever seen a foreigner lose their identity when they visit India? They remain true to their roots. But when Indians go abroad, they often change their attire, their habits, their very essence, forgetting who they are in the pursuit of adapting to foreign norms. This cannot continue if we are to preserve our rich culture and heritage.

If we want to protect and nurture India's future, we need to recognize the importance of our leaders. Shri Narendra Modi and Yogi Adityanath are indispensable in this regard.

Achievements of Prime Minister Narendra Modi's Government

Since Prime Minister Narendra Modi assumed office in May 2014, and later in his second term from May 2019, India has seen unprecedented growth and transformation. His vision for India, encapsulated in the slogan "Sabka Saath, Sabka Vikas, Sabka Vishwas," has steered the nation toward inclusive development and governance without corruption.

Under his leadership, India has witnessed the world's largest healthcare program—**Ayushman Bharat**—benefiting over 50 crore Indians by providing affordable and quality healthcare. The Lancet magazine has lauded the program for addressing India's healthcare needs. Moreover, India's **Jan Dhan Yojana** has ensured financial inclusion for millions, with over 35 crore accounts opened, providing the unbanked with access to financial services.

Through the **Pradhan Mantri Ujjwala Yojana**, more than 7 crore households, primarily women, now have access to clean cooking fuel. The **Swachh Bharat Mission** has also drastically improved sanitation, ensuring that 99% of India now has access to toilets, saving lives and improving public health across the nation.

Major Welfare Schemes:

1. **Pradhan Mantri Kisan Samman Nidhi** – This scheme provides direct income support to farmers, with the government allocating Rs 87,000 crore annually for their welfare.

2. PM Garib Kalyan Anna Yojana – This initiative ensured that no one went hungry during the pandemic, with food grains distributed free of charge to over 80 crore people.

3. Pradhan Mantri Awas Yojana – More than 1.25 crore houses have been built for the homeless, fulfilling the vision of "Housing for All."

4. Pradhan Mantri Shram Yogi Mandhan Yojana – Over 42 crore unorganized sector workers now have pension coverage, ensuring economic security for the most vulnerable sections of society.

Infrastructure Development:

India has also seen immense strides in infrastructure development. The UDAN (Ude Desh Ka Aam Nagrik) scheme has made air travel accessible to the common man, while the construction of highways, railways, and airports has accelerated. India's roads have become safer, and the introduction of bullet trains will further enhance the nation's connectivity.

Technological Advancements and Industrial Growth:

The **Make in India** initiative has successfully turned India into a global manufacturing hub. From just 2 mobile manufacturing units in 2014, the number has skyrocketed to 122 by 2019. GST

(Goods and Services Tax) has brought about a unified tax system, which simplified the business environment, improving India's ease of doing business ranking from 142 to 77.

Fostering a Clean, Green India:

Under Modi's leadership, India is also making great strides in environmental conservation. The government has laid out ambitious renewable energy targets, focusing on solar and wind energy. The **Namami Gange Programme**, aimed at cleaning the Ganga River, has been a landmark initiative for the environment.

Yogi Adityanath's Governance in Uttar Pradesh:

The achievements under Chief Minister Yogi Adityanath in Uttar Pradesh are equally impressive. His administration has prioritized law and order, ensuring that people of all communities, regardless of religion, feel safe and secure. The development of over 45 lakh houses, the construction of 2.61 crore toilets, and the implementation of welfare schemes such as **Ayushman Bharat**, benefiting 35% of the Muslim population in Uttar Pradesh, demonstrate his commitment to inclusive development.

The **Uttar Pradesh Skill Development Policy** has made the state a leader in promoting vocational skills and self-employment. The **Mukhyamantri Apprenticeship Protsahan Yojana** and **Yuva Entrepreneurship Development Campaign (YOUTH)** are helping the youth of the state create their own businesses and become self-reliant.

Yogi Adityanath's administration has also made remarkable strides in improving the law and order situation in the state. The establishment of 41 new police stations, the recruitment of over 1.37 lakh police personnel, and the implementation of the **Police Commissioner System** have brought about a significant reduction in crime, with robbery cases decreasing by 59.7% and murders falling by 47.09%.

Additionally, **Swachh Bharat Mission** has been a success in UP as well, making the state one of the top performers in cleanliness and sanitation. Uttar Pradesh is leading in milk, sugarcane, and food production and has garnered national recognition for its efforts in agriculture and rural development.

Conclusion:

Under the visionary leadership of Shri Narendra Modi and Chief Minister Yogi Adityanath, India has seen unprecedented transformation. From poverty alleviation to infrastructure development, education to healthcare, these leaders have prioritized the welfare of the people. As India prepares to embrace its status as a global leader, we must remain rooted in our culture and traditions while advancing in every field.

The journey is far from over, and with continuous efforts, India will not just be a Vishwaguru but also a beacon of progress, equality, and security for the world.

This version includes more of the key government initiatives and their impact while highlighting the cultural importance of maintaining India's identity. Let me know if you want to expand further or focus on any specific area!

.6.

Vishwaguru

In the pages of history, our country India is called the Vishwa Guru, which clearly means that the one who teaches the world or the teacher of the whole world, because the ancient economy of india, politics and the knowledge of the people here was so rich that all the countries from the east to the west were convinced of our India.

India's claim to the title of Vishwa Guru is based on the ancient idea: Vasudhaiva Kutumbakam, the whole world is one family. We argue because we were the first to say this all over the world , and only we follow these precepts, so we are uniquely qualified to become world gurus.

Seeing the prosperity and wealth of India, the foreigners became so greedy that they had to invade India so that they could fill their hungry stomachs with the wealth of India.

In making our country India a vishwaguru, the wise great men of that time have contributed a lot to whom we will be indebted forever.

The India of that time was self-sufficient as well as being a Vishwaguru , because it was our country India that invented many things. As if some of them are as follows –

Zero:-

Counting of mathematics is the gift of our India, so it has also been said that "when my India gave zero, then the world came to count".

In 628 AD, a scholar and mathematician named Brahmagupta, for the first time defined the principles of zero, followed by the great mathematician and astronomer Aryabhatta who used zero in the decimal system which was Indian.

Total:-

The tradition of yoga is very ancient and originated thousands of years ago. It is believed that yoga has been done ever since the civilization started. That is, yoga was born long before the oldest religions or beliefs were born.

In yoga, Lord Shiva is considered to be "Adi Yogi" and "Adi Guru".

After Lord Shankar, it is believed to be the beginning of yoga from the Vedic sages and munis. Later Krishna, Mahavira and Buddha expanded it in their own way. Patanjali then gave it a streamlined shape. This form was later expanded by the Siddhapanth, Shaivapanth, Nathpanth, Vaishnava and Shakta sects in their own ways.

Physiotherapy & Surgery:-

From the classical evidence, the original source of surgery is found in the Vedas, where the two vaidyas of heaven, Ashvinikumaras, after indra, agni and som devta, are counted. They have both physiotherapy and surgical functions. In order to remove the ailments of the body and to provide new eyes and new organs in case of fracture, a prayer has been offered to The AshwiniKumaras. If urine is blocked in the ureter, bladder and kidneys, there is a mention of surgical or otherwise exhaling the uterus. Similarly, in the Atharvaveda

, prayers have been offered to the medicine that heals the damaged, abscess, ulcers, broken or severed bones, repairs the amputated limb, heals the detached meat marrow. There are mentions of treatments such as bandage for bleeding, piercing for apchi (a disease of the gland of the throat), etc. It is described that during the time of Lord Buddha, a doctor named Jivatak successfully performed major surgeries in the area of karoti and abdominal.

Removing the head of Dadhichi and transplanting the horse's head in its place and then removing it and putting the real head, giving light to the blind eyes of Rizrashwad, re-inserting the severed head of the yajna, removing the leprosy of the shrava and giving him a long life, making the room a young man again, giving the old chyavan a new man again, giving the old chyavan a new man again, The removal of Vamdev from the mother's womb, etc., all these are also examples of surgery.

The foundation of ayurvedic surgery in a well-organized and classical manner was laid by

Indra's disciple Dhanvantri. Dhanvantri's disciple Sushruta developed this scripture as a holistic one and gave it a practical form. Even at that time, the field of surgery was normal physical surgery and vertical diseases and surgeries (i.e., diseases of the eye disease, nose, throat, ear, etc., and the surgery thereof) were considered separately in the shalakya branch of Ashtanga Ayurveda.

Astrology:-

Jyotish or The Jyotish theme is as ancient as the Vedas. In ancient times, the subject of studying planets, constellations and other celestial bodies was called Jyotish. About its mathematics part, it can be said very clearly that there are clear calculations in the Vedas about it. Information about the resulted part comes much later.

The number of manuscripts of astrology composed by Indian masters is more than one lakh. In ancient times, mathematics and geotish were synonyms, but later they became three parts.

(1) Tantra or theory - to acquire and determine the motions and constellations of planets by mathematics.
(2) Hora – which was related to the making of a coil. It had three subdivisions. A- Jataka, B-Yatra, C-Marriage.
(3) Branch – This was a wide section containing details of omen testing, symptom testing and future indication. What was known to these three skandhas

(tantra-hora-branch) was called 'kodipparag'.

There are mainly two parts in the system or theory, one consisting of the calculation of the planets, etc., and the other consists of values related to the beginning of creation, round thought, machine and chronology. The system and the principle cannot be kept separate at all. Among the characteristics of siddhanta, tantra and karana is that the idea of planetarind in which kalpadi or creation is from creation, the principle in which there is from mahayugadi, the system which is from the great age and which has a character (as from the beginning of kaliyuga) is called karana. Looking only from the point of view of planetary counts, there is no difference between these three. The cases of siddhanta, tantra or karana granth in which the idea of planetarind resides are as follows, respectively:

1-Medium Rights 2-Clear Rights 3-Tri-Question Rights 4-Chandra Lien 5-Surya Lien6-Shadyadhikar 7-Udayastadhikar 8-Shringontadhikar 9-Planetary Rights 10-Right of The Right to Travel

'Astrology' gives the following meaning- Vedaang Astrology Siddhant Astrology or Mathematics Astrology Fruitful AstrologyAnkshology

Sanskrit:-

The history of Sanskrit language is very old. The oldest Sanskrit scriptures received in the present time are the ऋgveda, which is a creation of at least 2,500 BC. Sanskrit (Sanskritam) is a language of the Indian subcontinent. It is also known as Devvani or Surbharati. It is the oldest language in the world. Sanskrit is an Indo-Aryan language that is a branch of the Indo-European language family. Modern Indian languages like Gujarati Hindi, Bangla, Marathi, Sindhi, Punjabi, Nepali, etc., originated from it. All these languages also include the Romani language of the European Banjaras. Almost all the scriptures related to the Vedic religion have been written in

Sanskrit. Many important texts of Buddhism (especially Mahayana) and Jainism have also been written in Sanskrit. Even today, most of the yagnas and pujas of Hinduism take place in Sanskrit.

Apart from all this, there are many inventions which have been made by our country India, which have been stolen by the foreign invaders and presented in their own language and shown to be their own.

.7.

Protector of Hinduism

For several days, the "so-called" Hindu nationalist faction has run an undeclared campaign against Modi. These people are very knowledgeable and consider themselves to be the greatest pioneers of Hindutva. Most of the time, but sometimes I read his post, then it seems that he had formed the Modi government and that too only because Modi will work only for Hindutva and he will not develop nor will he greet on the festivals of any other religion.

And in just 5 years, if you declare the country as a Hindu nation, then all the problems of this country will end on their own. And going a little further than this, it is found that in 4 years, the Modi government has done nothing for Hindutva but has worked against Hindutva. Because their posts will not mention any development work, nor will there ever be any mention of any work which is Hindu at the centre, on the contrary, these people keep trying to justify the present events from their own point of view by integrating it with the other on the basis of old stories by ignoring it from the end of the past. By the way, the work that Modi did in the interest of Hindutva has always been silent on these works and will remain silent even further because they have only to oppose.

The work done by the Modi government and other BJP governments in the Hindu interests is something like this.

** Ban on cow slaughter, along with the release of Aseemanand Sadhvi Pragya, the release of Colonel Purohit also took place in this government. And all of them were put in jail for many years by the Congress because of saffron terrorism.*

** The work of cleaning and beautification of the ghats of Banaras, a major centre of Hindutva philosophy and spirituality, was carried out.*

** Ayodhya and Mathura were given the status of municipal*

corporations so that these two cities could be properly developed which were neglected till today. This will only benefit the visitors who come here and the people here.

** Construction of Mansarovar Bhawan in Ghaziabad and doubling the amount of people going on Mansarovar Yatra from UP.*

** New route to Kailash opened from China and increased funds to be given.*

** The reconstruction of Kedarnath and the highway connecting the Charo Dham Yatra are being constructed in such a way that it remains for a long time and it is easy for people to reach here as well as the risk of life is reduced.*

** Constructed a rail route to the nearest to Vaishno Devi.*

** Connecting all religious places as a circuit and arranging* funds for travel in a *half-BJP-ruled states.*

** Increased budget of Ardh-Kumbh.*

** A grand Diwali was celebrated for the first time in Ayodhya, Uttar Pradesh.*

** The construction of the "Ramayana Circuit" began in Ayodhya and there was an ongoing Ram Leela which was once on the verge of closure due to lack of funds during the Akhilesh government' time, for which the Yogi government arranged funds.*

** Apart from this, during the Akhilesh government, when DJs* *were banned at the time of Kanvad Yatra and at the time of Holi, they were removed by the Yogi government and the unwritten ban on celebrating Janmashtami at police stations was also removed.*

** This was also the first time that holi and jumma were together, even when the prayer time was postponed.*

** Initiatives for cow protection and efforts towards construction of gau shalas were initiated. But of course, its speed is slow and the expected results have not come out.*

Freedom from the stain of saffron terrorism also came during the time of this government.

The Congress which was bringing a minority communally targeted bill in which if a majority does something on the minority, then strict action and on the contrary, the minority was being given the responsibility in it, it went into cold storage and now some people are wanting that if Modi did nothing for Hindutva, then bring anyone and then it will come up with such a new bill, then it will be understood that Modi has not done anything for Hindutva.

What did you do for Hindutva?

** Yoga, part of the Hindutva philosophy, was recognised internationally and yoga day was celebrated on June 21.*

** Presenting Gita to most heads of state.*

** If Modi ji includes Japan's PM Shinzo Abe in the aarti of Mother Ganga ji, then it is fine. Going beyond that, Shinzo Abe should do the aarti yourself and apply tilak, that too is fine. After that, the Muslim President of Afghanistan, Hamid Karzai, went to the Golden Temple, then once again Modi ji's wah-wah, another Christian Australian Prime Minister was taken to Akshardham temple by Modi himself sitting in the metro.*

** When the temple was built in Abu Dhabi, the Muslim rulers came there and gave land for the temple and cooperated in the construction of the temple.*

** Presented Gita to many heads of state. So he has also gone to many temples in foreign countries and in the country also in different states, he is the only PM to go to such a temple, due to which the Congress had to change its strategy and tell Rahul as Janeu.Dhari and even Rahul is going to temples.*

While this is Rahul who once said that 'people go to temples to tease girls'.

* On the other hand, the girls were worshipped at the time of Navdurga at the Chief Minister's residence and Rashtrapati Bhavan in Uttar Pradesh.

** Right from the SC order, but this government abolished the Haj subsidy.*

** Sanskrit was given the status of official language in Uttarakhand.*

** Yoga and Ayurveda were promoted at the central and state level. The number of their colleges was increased and the number of medical colleges of Ayurveda was also increased.*

** It was only after the arrival of the Modi government that zakir naik's peace foundation was banned, action was taken, illegal NGOs were closed down which were involved in anti-Hindu activities, missionaries and Islamic institutions were exposed!*

** It was during Modi's time that Shrikant Purohit, Sadhvi Pragya, PSI Banjara and former MLA Maya Kodnani were brought out of jail who were somewhere implicated in the heinous conspiracy of false 'Hindu atrocity'!*

** No one has been tortured in this government just because he is a Hindu, which is the biggest thing.*

What more do you want than those who are opposing Modi only in the name of Hindutva?

In the first few temples, there were terrorist attacks but in 4 years there were only threats, but it is also a success of this government not to allow any such attack to be carried out before.

Modi's karkarkar gave ladder entry to all 'Hindu refugees' in India.

In 8 states, Hindus got the status of a minority, due to the efforts of this government.

Now, if someone should say that what is joyous about this, it is not right that hindus became a minority in eight states.

So the great thing is that the Hindu minority happened during the time of the previous governments, but it did not get the rights and facilities that it should have already got because of being a minority. The government made efforts in this direction and the matter went to the Supreme Court and the government won in this direction.

The UP government is making fresh efforts for the development of Chitrakoot.

All the things I remembered were told that the government did for The Hindu interests.

But the point here is that if it is not Modi, then who?

They will bring the Congress which says in the Supreme Court that Ram is a fictional person and who tried hard to demolish the Ram Setu. And so even the Shankaracharya was put in jail for many years.

The rest of the saffron terrorism, calling Batala House a fake encounter, Sadhvi Pragya , colonel purohit in jail, trying to bring in a minority-targeted bill and trying their best to stall the Ram temple hearing a few days ago.

Will you bring the soft? Who had opened fire on the Karsevaks. Who had stopped the two and a half Kosi and Panch Kosi yatras. Whose government had crossed all limits of Muslim appeasement.

Or will they bring Mamata Banerjee? The lesson about them is to know how kind and compassionate they are.

Who will bring or who will come as an alternative to Modi by standing up as an anti-Hindutva opponent with just a few incidents?

Till 2014, there were 44,000 Shakhas of the RSS, which has now become 58,000.

And at one point of time, during Akhilesh's government, social media was buzzing with reports of RSS men being beaten up by the police in Agra.

The Rashtriya Gokul Mission was launched by this Government. Just now, when Modi ji went to the mosque in Indonesia and put on a green shawl there, this section was the most severed on that too.

But he never tried to know what Modi ji came to do there.

There is a temple in the country with the largest Muslim population.

Its name is Prambanan Temple. The Prambanan temple located in Central Java is dedicated to Lord Shiva, Lord Vishnu and Lord

Brahma. This temple is the famous and largest Hindu temple in Indonesia. The special thing about this huge Hindu temple is that along with the Tridevas, there are also temples of their vehicles. This temple has been declared a World Heritage Site by UNESCO.

In Modi's visit to Indonesia, an agreement was reached between the Archaeological Survey of India for the world cultural heritage of this temple. But everyone was silent about it.

A few days ago, the BJP government in UP banned liquor in the pilgrimage areas of Mathura.

Barsana, Gokul, Govardhan, Nandgaon, Radhakund and Baldev in the district were declared as prohibition zones. Similarly, Nagar Panchayat Govardhan, Radha Kund, Nandgaon and Baldev have been declared as holy shrines on March 22, this year. 29 lakhs for the newly built International Ram Katha Museum and Art Gallery in Faizabad. Being in UP, the BJP government here is aware of the work of Hindu interests.

In other BJP-ruled states of the rest, similar works will take place, they can be added to this list according to their own. Allahabad was renamed as Prayagraj.

These are some examples of other states where there is no BJP government.
Look at West Bengal, where it is Ram Navami or Durga Puja or the Sangh's program, the government bans all this, then the ban is lifted from the court.

In Kerala, Vami Kangi cuts cows on the road and eats it.

Tipu Sultan Jayanti is celebrated in Karnataka. The decision is now for you to do it yourself who say day and night that what the BJP has done for Hindutva.

So these were the things that Modi and the BJP did for the Hindus, but some people never saw this work nor did they discuss it.

All they remember is:

'Ram Mandir', 'Article 370' and 'Common Civil Code!'

On these three issues, big posts are written every day to surround Modi and people are told that look Modi has not done anything for Hindus, and development will not work, everyone will be kept captivated.

Now, if we talk about these 3 key points, the BJP in its 2014 manifesto has first written in the headline "Protecting Indian Culture and Heritage" that

1. *All options of Ram Temple will be explored within the ambit of the Constitution.*

2. . *While deciding on ram setu, its cultural heritage and*

thorium reserves will be taken into account.

3. *Cows and cow progeny will be protected.*

4. *The purity of ganga ji and its uninterrupted flow will be ensured.*

5. *A Uniform Civil Code inspired by the best traditions and as per the spirit of the Constitution.*

The first issue is 'Ram Temple'. The ram temple has been heard in the SC for the last 7-8 years, but the real momentum has come only last year under the leadership of CJI Dipak Misra ji.

Otherwise, how many CJIs went away and the case remained the same. Justice Khehar had also offered to mediate outside the court but before that the hearing was in a way closed. Subramanian Swamy's petition was heard expeditiously and it was expected that a decision would also come before October.

But then Sibal said in the SC that its decision should come after the elections and in the end, an attempt was made to put the CJI under pressure by initiating the impeachment process.

If we look at the whole case and analyse it, there was no progress in the Ram Janam Bhoomi case during the time of the Congress. Even in the first two years of the BJP, there was no significant initiative in this direction, but later on, the efforts of Sri inside and outside the court and the support of shia people to the temple were the result of the efforts of the government. The rest of the matter is in the court and it is in the interest of the country to be solved by him and it will not happen, but even if it happens by 1%, then the government will bring an ordinance and build the temple.

Those who are talking about bringing an ordinance now should also keep in mind the politics of other parties, which will make it public all over the country tomorrow that the BJP does not respect judicial procedures.

The second issue is 'Section 370'. The culmination also started at the same time when the BJP's lawyer asked the SC to clarify the 35A constitutional status in the SC. Because this is what has to start from this, otherwise everyone knew about 370, but no one knew about 35 A. It is true that it also did not reach the end, but it will not be easy to reach such a quick conclusion. And it may take another 10-12 years to finish it because the government will end it only when the Valley is completely calm and there is peace in Jammu and Kashmir and a consensus will be formed on this.

The third issue is of the 'Common Civil Code'

On the Common Civil Code, the BJP government has given the 'Uniform Civil Code' Bill to the law panel in 2017 and the discussion on the same is ongoing. It will take time, he has earlier initiated their equal rights among Muslims, in which triple talaq was abolished and the next hearing is going on Halala. This will make the road ahead of the Common Civil Code easier.

The rest of me expected the Modi government to be more vocal on the Rohingya issue and on the political killings taking place in West Bengal, but here the government's attitude was disappointed. But still, apart from this government, no other government or political party can be expected in this regard. Now, there is no shortage of those who call Modi's development nonsense only on the basis of Hindutva. He says that the government should work on those 3 issues, the rest of the development does not mean anything to anyone. Nor does it matter.

So, all of these are just a simple question that these people will live without electricity and water for just one day? When there is no electricity throughout the day, the mobile will also not be charged, then how will they post Hindutva? If the light goes off for just a few hours, the man starts to cry. If there is no water for one day, then think about what will happen? If a road of 5 km is found to travel full of potholes, then the meaning of development will be understood.

Go to the water crisis that is there in Shimla right now and ask them if they want these 3 issues or do they want water? Everything has to be taken along and with balance. This is a matter of understanding, if religion also increases and protects it, then on the other hand, there is development, only then the country and society can progress.

The rest of Modi was considered by these people as Hindu pride, after 2002. He did not come to convince himself that he should consider him as the protectors of Hindu interests.

Even before the elections in the AAP court, he had spoken about the Quran and laptop in one hand of the Muslims, and he had already contested the elections on the Gujarat development model, just said that he would not do the politics of appeasement.

This was the case for you to understand people, so why are you blaming others for it?

There is doubt among the people and it is neither right for Hindutva nor for the country.

It is very important to keep the balance according to the time.

Otherwise, on the one hand, Trump continues to fulfill his national policies, but people are still not happy with him and Trump is also being isolated at the international level.

And in the end, let's assume that this government has done nothing for the Hindus.

But it's also that nothing has been done against hindus!

Isn't that enough, then?

But all this will not be seen, these so-called nationalists will not want to understand the people anymore.

These chests are saying that "Modi" is anti-Hindu, i.e, a clear lie.

Simplified Version of the actual

A Call for Cultural Preservation

In the modern age, the line between embracing globalization and losing one's cultural identity has become blurred. We are constantly witnessing a significant shift in how people, especially the youth, perceive their heritage. Take, for instance, the growing popularity of a Pakistani song, "Pasoori," which has captivated a significant portion of the Indian subcontinent. Around 60% to 70% of citizens are listening to it, yet only 5% to 10% understand its exact meaning. Similarly, people have started drifting away from

Indian music, preferring K-Pop, English, and even Pakistani music, while slowly forgetting the cultural significance of our own languages and musical traditions.

In this era, where Western influence dominates, we seem to have forgotten the essence of our own culture. While we are listening to songs from foreign lands, the legends of Indian music—whether it's classical maestros or modern icons—are being neglected. It's becoming increasingly clear that we are forgetting the beauty and importance of our own traditions, and blindly following trends that originate from elsewhere.

Is Our Culture Worth Forgetting?

The question I want to raise is simple: Is our culture not worthy of respect? Is it so inferior that we must abandon it in favor of foreign practices? If our culture, our language, our traditions are so great, why are we forsaking them for something alien?

Back in May 2022, I observed a disturbing trend in India—people were forgetting their roots. The vibrancy of Indian culture, our traditions, and the pride we once had in speaking our mother tongues seemed to be fading. In response,

I published posts advocating for #MyCultureMyFame and calling for a boycott of K-Pop, urging people to reconnect with their true identity as Indians. However, instead of support, my posts were humiliated and disregarded by many, which only strengthened my resolve to take a different route. This led to the idea of writing a book that celebrates India, Hinduism, our government, and our political leaders—Shri Narendra Modi and Shri Yogi Adityanath—who are tirelessly working to restore the pride of our nation.

The Truth I Discovered

Up until the age of 10, I was taught that India belonged to all faiths. I believed in unity and harmony, and I respected all communities. But as I grew older, I embarked on a journey of understanding India's true history. I studied the past with a critical eye, and it became clear to me that India has always been, and will always be, a land rooted in Hinduism. It is the first religion that emerged in Asia, and the first language spoken was Sanskrit, which has influenced every other language in the world. I realized that all languages have evolved from Sanskrit, making it the foundation of human communication.

The Role of English and Foreign Practices

While English has become a necessary language for global business and employment, I find it concerning how we have prioritized foreign languages over our own. We learn English to find employment in foreign countries, but have you ever seen a foreigner in India learn Hindi or adopt Indian customs in their education? No, they continue to use their native languages, wear their own clothes, and celebrate their own food. Why is it that we, the citizens of India, feel the need to abandon our language, our food, and our culture to fit into a mold that is not our own?

Another common practice we follow blindly is wearing ties and jeans—clothes that were introduced to us by the British.

Yet, we have adopted them as part of our daily attire without questioning their origins. Similarly, the traditional sari, a beautiful Indian garment that has been worn for centuries, has become less common. Women today are opting for Western-style clothing such as t-shirts, jeans, and other foreign attire.

This raises a question—**Is the sari so inferior that we must abandon it in favor of Western clothing?**

It's crucial that we, as Indians, rediscover our cultural identity and take pride in our heritage. We must begin by questioning why we are discarding our traditions and whether we have fully embraced the beauty and richness of our own culture. It's time to acknowledge that India's history, language, and values are worthy of celebration and preservation. The future of India lies in its ability to blend the best of modernity with the rich traditions that have stood the test of time.

Let us return to our roots, protect our culture, and wear our identity with pride.

www.ingramcontent.com/pod-product-compliance
Lightning Source LLC
LaVergne TN
LVHW021141160826
845679LV00023B/1996

9798887721170